Whispers of the Heart
A Collection of Poems

Whispers of the Heart
A Collection of Poems

Veena Khurana

ZORBA BOOKS

ZORBA BOOKS

Publishing Services by Zorba Books, March 2020

Website: www.zorbabooks.com
Email: info@zorbabooks.com

Cover design © Sithesh
Copyright © *Veena Khurana*

ISBN 978-93-90011-05-6
E-book ISBN 978-93-90011-06-3

Zorba Books Pvt. Ltd. (opc)
Sushant Arcade,
Next to Courtyard Marriot,
Sushant Lok 1, Gurgaon – 122009, India

Acknowledgement

I would like to thank the Almighty for having given me the insight to explore an unknown path. "You the omnipresent, omnipotent Almighty" gave me the power to believe in my passion, without your blessings, this achievement would not have been possible.

I owe my deep sense of my gratitude to my children ''Alishaa and Joshoa '', who are more like my buddies; and have been equally excited by this quest to my dream. They have been my true source of inspiration. I wish to thank every person, who has somehow or the other has touched and inspired me. I express my gratitude to the zorba publishing team for all the guidance.

Preface

Writing this collection of poems has been a humbling experience. While writing each piece of poem, it's been an awakening of mind, heart and stirring of emotions. Each poem opened the doors to the emotions buried in the nest of my heart. The myriad moods and experience of life got a sparkle and took a shape of poetry, as the exquisite words gushed forth on a piccc of paper.

The personal ebb and flow of emotions has helped me to compose and tear the veil of darkness and in a flash sometime I have been able to stir up new insight into life joining the fragmented pieces of thoughts with an arousal of emotions in a rhythmical lyric. The most rewarding moment of my life has been a sense of elation and satisfaction after the completion of each poem.

Human mind is always travelling, flickering and inconsistent whereas the heart in its solitary isolation lives in a dream world of its own. While peering secretly in a solitary moment on to this fertile land of dream world, new ideas for poems were conceived and elevated my understanding of life. Poetry is having a dialogue to ones inner calling, an explosion of emotions woven into words.

Life's journey is a mixed bag of joy and sorrow, count each step and count your blessings, if you love someone express it...you never know when they will be gone. The poem "Dear father I love you" has been written after I lost him. It's my way of expressing my love for him of which I was never so open about it and after his death the floodgates of emotions flowed hence giving birth to "Dear father I love you". When death cast its shadow. Each of us bows down to the ways of almighty, realizing this there originated "The end", "Dirge".

The daily doses of introspection and communion with inner self has reinforced and strengthened the positivity, hence giving birth to "Painting a life", "Fragility of relationship". As I watched people scurrying around with their baggage of fears and bundles of raw emotions, I try to infuse some tranquility and equanimity of mind in their fast paced life with the poems like "Time to say goodbye" and "The trapped soul". There are poems of hopes,desire,nature and life poems.

While relaxing late night outside under the spell of full moon, I was totally mesmerized and the wings of imagination soared with its unbridled fantasies and the romance at night began, giving birth to "Romance at night". Love is a feeling of exaltation. In the poem "Willowy lass" the nature woos its ladylove by praising and extols the woman while draping her passionately with all its beauty.

Poetry is to be read several times as its meaning lies much deeper requiring a thoughtful pondering. It is "music in the words", a rhythm from the first word to the last word, delighting the mind and heart equally with its soft, delicate, lilting words. The musical words haunt the ears, quicken the senses and open the doors to the splendid beauty around. Poetry is the food that nourishes the starved soul. The main purpose of this book is to have a glimpse into a world of fantasy with new understanding and baring the soul tenderly, some of my poems are nude without any ornamental adjectives bringing alive the rawness of a seeker. Poems are a reflection of what you hold inside.

Last but not least, believe in the dictum "Know thyself", as most of us live the life and die, never really knowing the creative genius that lives within most of us. Hence the potential never finds an expression and outlet.

> "The best and the most beautiful things in the
> world cannot be seen or ever touched; they must
> be felt with heart."
>
> As told by HELEN KELLER

Content

A SONG TO LIVE

Echoes a tuneless melancholy strain.

Writhes and whimpers the song crying,
Crushed along with the dreams of tomorrow,
Sighs along with the shadows haunting,
Buried along with the hopes of tomorrow,
The song silenced without a sound,
Swallowed into distance unknown.

All I seek is my song back.

Of happy strain a song to live,
This is sung not in vain,
Soothes the heart in pain,
Wipes a tear of a sorrow laden eye,
The lilting grace that echoes cheerily,
In the secret hour the sweetness savored.

All I seek is a smile on my lips.

As the moon rides higher and higher,
To sing the song hand in hand with silver speckled glitter,
The sleeping dreams are streaked silvery,
Filling the heart with illusionary dreams,
That radiates the promised dreams,
To bring alive the dream of eternal ties,

All I seek are my dreams back

Unbidden and unbridled the song so wild,
Hugs the soul with a playful harmony
Rushes from the lips a rhythmic flow,
Kisses the cheek that dimples with delight,
The crimson glow hugs the face so pale,
A rhapsody of melodious strain.

All I seek is the broken chord to mend again.

The morning star sings a cheerful note,
Mingled in the fragrance of a glory of the spring,
Sung in harmony with gentle breeze,
The haunting autumn fades away,
The wintry tears dry away,
Sings the life a promise of sunny days.

All I want the promise of sunny days.

Singing ever for days to emerge,
Unfolding the path to eternal bliss,
Embarking upon with a song of happiness,
A farewell to sorrow laden heart.
All I want to color the canvas of my life,
Where smiles each moment to perfume the life heavenly.

All I want to soak in the happier days ahead.

ALONE NOW

Crippled with loneliness, to an endless walk,
Befriending my loneliness in a valley of sadness,
Selfish you were to walk alone with your last breath,
To an unseen nothingness of unknown destination,
Where none dare to venture,
With their heart beat strong,

My heart is like a vast desert,
Footprints of your memories etched in the sands of time,
Watering each breath with tears rolling,
Vultures sneak to prey on memories, scratch the wound,
oozing pain,
I try to foil their very attempt,
Nursing my wound to nurture my future,

My day starts with you in my each breath,
Gasping in the throbbing memories alive,
Scathing wound of my innermost core,
For the world around,
You were just a name about,
For me you were my only world around,

In the eerie silence with my grief alone, this has no home
to reside,
Choking me in the saltiness of my tears,
Drinking lonliness, to be high,

Trying to reach a destination shrouded, no one knows,
Whispering a name in a silky rhapsody,
A secret rendezvous in a la la land,
I hear, I see, a waving silhouette,

With a beckoning sigh,
I stretch my arm far and beyond,
The scent of you I still breathe in me,
Pushing away the demons of loneliness,
To walk a path of bitter sweet togetherness,
But the sojourn lasting, not even a fraction of second,

An icy cold fear numbs a soul torn apart,
The parched bleakness of heart's despair,
As the visions of togetherness gathers dust,
Togetherness thrives only in the graveyard of memories,
Sunrise and sunset of each day, will smoothly pass to an
eternal path,
Leaving me abandoned with my grief riddled heart,

Wearing a mask,
A savior to my life's trudge,
Scattered I am with broken smiles,
Hiding a torment behind a mask of smile,
Crushed within with tons of miseries,
I am deceived by god's skillfully planned destiny,

Begging each star to blink some silvery promise,
Hugging my pillow tight,
To ward away the stubborn loneliness,

The warmth of my blood,
Lulls me to a deep slumber,
The night's shadow promise a silver lining,

Detached I am to the day's miseries trap,
Cocooned in the arms of my beloved,
Tonight I shall abandon all my aches,
My dreams of night are the future promise of all nights,
I have deceived the god's skillfully planned destiny,
My page of life holds every tear with a smile.

BEJEWELED PAPER

Violet jacaranda blossoms in a gossamer canopy,
Virgin blossoms meander through gentle breeze,
Unruly dominance of a gentle rainfall of jacaranda,
I am swathed in a lilac radiance,
Within myself a storm is brewing,
Sending the heart to dizzying high, is an innocent dainty lilac,
Lazy noontide fans my senses wild,
Aroused I am like no lover ever aroused,
Ripened youth of jacaranda blossom, leaning in lissome lilt,
The wafting fragrance teasing my thoughts with a persistence
cajoling,
Indolent forgetfulness and noontide solitude, a potent mixture,
Applauding my thoughts peppered with soul full musings,
A didgeridoo thrown in for a soul,
A jamboree of luminous sensations,
Raring to go, the words into an eclectic mélange,
Sensitive desires onto a musical potpourri,
Pristine poetry on sensitive path designed of poise and élan,
Perched above is a kingfisher, flaps its wings in delight,
Melodious babble of feathered friends in flight, pause in awe,
Adding grace to an unbridled reverie, a poetic drama dazzling
a placid paper,
A torrential downpour of fertile emotions, untamed,
Rhythmic frenzy on a quivering paper,
Forlorn not now is the paper, in an unifying spirit,
The mating of words in an orchestra, to a drunken sway,

Grace of each word lingers, making my heart tango,
Sunrays surges to color the words crimson,
Breathless is the breeze, sigh in admiration,
Each words sways in a pampered adulation,
Like a seductress out to seduce,
Between the lines there are oomph and sighs!
Sometime a whiff of sorrow and joy,
Drizzle of sadness takes a refuge in comfort of joy,
Blanks are filled with excitement for a lyrical word of a
next line,
Interwoven sensitive emotions in words,
A deep hunger wooed with fervor,
Shaping up a random poem in its purest form,
Blending into one another, is a celebration of words,
Love me; fondle me, the bejeweled paper on a passionate trail.

BETRAYAL

Lonesome ever,
Anguished soul of robbed sunshine,
Rhythmic mind of mournful song,
Seeks the heart the loved one,

Schizophrenic screams,
Cradling a bleeding day,
Maiming dreams of a dreaming soul,
Nibble at life until fed,

Soiled footpath of betrayal echoes,
Choking the heart shorn and woeful,
Desires wails, furtively slashing my share of happiness,
Hunger in depth for a longing caress,

Writhing wings of clipped heart,
Thats been butchered by a heart so cold,
Unfaithful promise breeds the gloom,
Stripped and naked, bleeding emotions on a thorny path,

Alone I sway, now in grief,
Vacant gazes, tomorrows wrapped in pain,
Disabled soul accompany my loneliness,
What I have gained is a tormented heart.

CACTUS

An abyss in a heart of abandoned cactus,
Am I pariah, hatred spewed?
Just a glance what I plead,
Agonizing longing of a bulbous stump,
Scalded by neglect,
Lonesome in a garden of rose blossoms,
Your glossy red petals what I envy,
I am ripe, bursting with love,
Did I prick you ever with my smile?
As you sway with your petals in rosy blush,
You stand in all your glory; I drink all your tears,
Lying awake day and night,
Like a sentinel to a rose garden,
Poets and lovers loathe my being,
Spikes are my barbed fence, protecting the gentleness within,
Dreaming ever to weave a story of rose and cacti unison,
The rhythmic winds make a rose dance in a maddening orgy,
Fluttering motion to a lifeless scatter,
Summer heat sucks the last bit of life,
And I have drunk all the summer rain,
In a deathly pallor as you perish on pregnant earth,
I too perish on the same ground,
There we will, bloom one in unison,
Enchanted moment will not elude,

2---I adorn a sunset of a peaceful resting,
Souls I meet are my lovers alone,
A proud blossom of a graveyard, all in my glory,
I am loved in all my ugliness,
Bees and butterflies visit when souls are in slumber,
The silent conversation I share with souls alone,
To make them whole in the canopy of darkness,
As they moan about their life spent,
I drink their sorrows of a life spent,
As they let their broken stars tell their tales.

CONFUSION

Salvation shakes as shrines are revered of pseudo prayers,
The wretched desperation of a muffled soul,
The orgy of bells in the wilderness of human stampede,
Provokes a cacophony of a mind haywire,
The tranquility broken amidst thousand questions,
Serpentine path, leads to nowhere,
Groping amidst in a jungle of thoughts,
The puzzling jig jag of lives reborn,
A fabric of life woven, unwoven hundredth times,
Confusion stalks to chase that elusive answer,
Weeding out thorns for a trail to alluring peace.

CRIES OF A TREE

Silent and solitary,
A stranger in a ruthless land,
Gnarled and twisted, eroded with no cares,
Standing barren with dried stump neglected,

The fiery sun with all its might,
And the piercing winds with strength to reckon,
Scorches and notches,
A feeble whimper breaks in a sigh, no one hears,

Gnaws gleefully the white ants,
The bleeding tree in a feeble attempt,
Screams and gasp is the last bit of strength,
A tale of woe is of no one's business,

The vultures oblige,
To scratch and clean with utmost care,
Their beaks and claws,
Leave behind a tale of their gory deeds,

Robbed of its might by the ravages of times,
Hollow in spirit with nothing to cheer,
Echoes a melancholy melody, a raspy cry of a tree,
The cold winds sucking away last whiff of warmth,

With a whiff of excitement,
To earn his next meal,
The woodcutter looks up and down,
Eyes so greedy and the axe so ready,

In a somber moment a fatal call is sounded,
My doom is mirrored in the ugly blaze,
My soul burns to warm a heart of a winter night,
And I am lost into a calculative demonic move.

DAWN

The dancing moon with roving eyes,
Flirted the night in the darkness,
Entangled in passion on the sly,

Mesmerized and enchanted,
The earth so drunk,
Embraced in a silvery mesh with a hold so tight.

Drowsy and yawning now the moon so tired,
Drifting away to a dreamy slumber,
Cradled by the arms of warm glow.

The millionth diamonds cluster together,
Forming a bed above the clouds,
Dreams the moon the starry dreams.

Softly and silently with a burning passion,
Wakes the dawn with the lids so heavy,
Roused and enchanted by the glory of morning passion.

The singing birds flock together,
To sing a lullaby to the dreaming moon,
That dreams of another night.

The streams so frozen in the stillness of silvery magic,
Now gushes forth with a golden dazzle,
Swirls and whirls around a water lily,

Lazily yawns a blossomed bud,
Kissing the golden ray in its lap,
Opens the bosom to the beetles so hungry.

Leaps and rises the heavenly air,
Fanning the petals of a matured bud,
Caress and sucks with a bellyful.

Filling itself with a fragrance so intoxicating,
Heavy and billowing is the breath so fragrant,
Spreading its fragrance with gay abundance,

Bathes the earth in the heavenly nectar,
Washing away the nights slumber,
Wakeful now with the song of morning glory.

Throbs the earth with a passion revived,
A passion setting the earth in a golden blaze,
Blushes the earth in a golden blaze.

DEAR FATHER –I LOVE YOU

I remember, I remember,
The glorious times of sunny days,
The piggy rides,
The look of pride, the twinkle in eyes,
When I lisped the word "papa",
The love that rocked the cradle with happiness,
The hands that toiled with every drop of sweat,
To fill my life with every drop of comfort,
The growing years missed no joy,
But a little sentence missed my lips.

Only if I had said "I love you papa"

The sunniest of sunny day is clouded by a grief so great,
The busiest of the busy day is empty,
With a vacuum so great,
If ever there was an earth so thirsty,
I would drown it with rainfall of tears,
If ever there was a pond so dry,
I would fill it with tears of sorrow.
Cried in silence of night,
Cried the hidden tears behind a mask of smile,
Cried the heart with dried tears

Only if I could touch you and say "I love you papa"

I look beyond that stretches to nothing,
The heart is helpless,
For having wasted the years gone by,
The gestures of love,
Gone unexpressed,
The unsaid word, a painful echo,
That stabs the heart with anguish,
Ringing loudly in the hush of night,
Tears of remorse flows from the heart,
Filling an ocean with guilt that overflows..

Only if I had said "I love you papa"

Somewhere there the heart knows,
You are there for me alone,
One amongst the twinkling star,
Shining and smiling,
Waiting and watching,
Whispering the words so soft,
"Not to cry the tears of sorrow",
"Not to cry the tears of remorse",
As I am at peace with my inner self,
The pain, the suffering,
Burnt with the ashes,
But the eyes that look up,
Are lost in the vast universe,
The heart knows,

That you wait for me,
To rock and welcome,
In your arms,
But until then,
I wait in despair.

DIRGE

Here chimes the distant bells,
Here sung the beckoning song,
Here lies the dreams fallen with unseen hopes,
Here I sleep the sleep of no waking,
Here I start the journey to another land,
The journey to final abode,
Put no flowers on,
But smell the fragrance of memories,
For that is freshly acquired possession never betraying a
heart ever,
Mourn not when I am gone,
For deep in your heart,
I sing a song of happiness for a happier tomorrow,
Shed not the tears of sorrow,
But relive the joyous times spent,
For that is something no vision can dim,
Miss me not,
For I will come in the dreams of your slumber,
To whisper softly the words of comfort,
Hug not the times gone by,
But embrace the promises of tomorrow,
For in my death I have promised a golden future for you,

Feed not the loneliness around,
For if the earthly moorings are cut,
But deep within I have come to live forever in your heart,
Bid me no farewell,
For if death closes all,
It opens the door to cherished times.

DIVINE HEALING

As my aimless eyes, vacant of its goal wonder,
Unknown angel sings a lullaby to unveil,
Rousing the soul to revel in shimmering dawn,
Haunting soft whispers of eternal bliss,
Distilled thoughts crystallizes heart,

Breaking the outer sheath unfurling a holy glow,
Of dancing images of divine omnipresent,
God's merciful wisdom let me ponder,
Trespassing a territory of sinful doer,
That is trapped in a mire of sins,

Yes, now I sway in ecstasy of your love,
Bathing me in fragrance of purity,
Life's folly succumbs with heaviness,
Falling into garbage of sin,
Slumbering soul wakes up to divine soul,

Yes, the pulsating strength of belief,
Towards my sacred infinity,
Moments conspire of mystic streams,
New vision smiles seducing senses to ultimate bliss,
Ensnarls senses in pure magic,

Mirroring the beckoning of my essence,
A journey through seasons of futile path,
Anger, hate dissolves with no remorse,
Pristine, unconditional love in unison with divine,
Oh! Beloved, I embrace you my lover divine,
Yes, I surrender to be a part of you, my divine.

DREAMS UNVEILED

Heavily laden sky of its sensuous night garb,
Auspicious guests of night arrive with equal panache,
Stars and moon ogle with a naughty twinkle,
At my travail of night's slumber,
A nascent dreamer, with my dreams of wanderlust,
Traveler of unseen calling, a willful surrender to a
beckoning charm,
Striking a chord,
Dream's lust unveiled,
Buried jewels of a flawless night come alive,
An enchantress, not awake to the conscious surroundings,
Day's tyranny, lifeless with no waking,
I lay bare, intoxicated with a hold so firm,
Naked to wander through all seasons,
A maddening frolic of frivolous wander,
Night's canopy of magical mesh, to revel on,
Magnificence dreams drape an infatuated quest,
I tremor to the night's scent of sensual longing,
The million stars blinking away the pathway to a velvety
black sky,
Escorting me to my beloved's trail,
Waltzing now in a mature thirst,
With the swooning moon in its reflection, on a silver trail,
Longing of unknown exploration in a dreamy trance,

Burning passion sees secrets of remote mystique,
Resplendent impossible within my reach,
Not in the grasp of day's intruder,
The nights shadow veiling a wicked game,
Silent witnesses are my pillow and bed, has unveiled my
sweetest dream.

ECSTASY

When the heart beckons,
The mind surrenders,
A slave of romance,
Bows to the heart,
The hunger of the heart,
Maketh the two moan in ecstasy,
    There is a storm beneath all the calm,
    Night is a slave to a passion's will,
    Will power flee to destination unknown,
    Heart does not tame a love that overflows,
    Chaotic emotions of two locked in one,
    Cheek to cheek,
    Body to body,
    In that sanctity no air dares to pass,
    Shedding all, their social grace,
    Tonight there is no mask to wear,
    Screams and ecstasy in a harmonious muffle,
    The blazing embrace threatens to burn the two,
    Melting like candle wax,
Ebbing and rising of emotions,
To a romantic frenzy,
And the mating of lightening,
To a thundering cloud,
A rain of melody,
Quenching the two love laden souls.

EMOTIONAL BAGGAGE

My life's drama locked in years,
Relentless pursuit of a heart in an old carcass,
Unlocking now to wade through years,
Meandering pathways of life's charade,
Uphill to downhill, a zigzag prance,

Hopes and regrets,
Tears of happiness and sorrow all melt together,
In the junk of yesterday, a mangled heap,
Weighing down on robust years crammed,
A crowded space, where I do not belong,

My foolish eyes were blind to the bullying of emotions,
Loyal years puffed up of toxic intentions,
With all the baggage I was chained,
Sometime with ribbons of silk,
Sometime with chains that scarred my heart,

What weighed me down was not mine to carry,
Love or hatred, a destructive motive of the same,
I need no flower to decorate myself, which rots with
passing time,
The kisses were a contract, a lure of futile emotional drama,
Where I burnt with too much of emotional baggage,

To travel light, I bid goodbye to emotional baggage,
Living full now, to fall in love with less and less,
Time and time, is now running less,
The remains of leftovers to be indulged upon,
With bare necessities worthy of time,
Then to return home without any baggage,

I need no cacti growing in my heart's garden,
I live in the spring of my heart,
That I shall not bargain with autumn,
In the silent space within me is a temple,
In that hush no emotion invades, until my last season,

Now not knowing,
How many countless breaths to breathe,
A remnant of insults still jeers my heart's fragile bed,
Each breath releasing a worthless baggage,
Exhaling turbulent emotions that has raged long,
Feeble wheeze, a weightless lullaby to sooth.

ETERNAL

Gone are the moments,
Gone are the days,
Gone are the years,
That I am never to walk,
Swallowed by time,
Clouded by dust,
But what lives forever,
In the loving nest, will throb forever,
Where one sees the other,
Where one hears the other,
Where one smells the other,
Where one feels the other,
In the loving nest,
In the nest of my heart,

Years will come,
Years will go,
Seasons will come,
Seasons will go,
But I will be alive,
To keep you alive,
In the loving nest,
In the nest of my heart,
Where I smile for you,

Where I sing for you,
Where the smell of you,
Fragrant with love,
Puts an arm,
An arm around me,

With every dawn,
With every dusk,
I in my dreams,
Will nestle together,
Together with you, in the nest of my heart,
Where the beat of your heart,
Is a beat of my heart,
In the nest of my heart,
Where no winter frosts the heart,
Where the midnights glimmer,
The noon's glow,
Will burn together to a heightened passion,
Where you and I will breathe as one,
Together as one in one breath.

FIRST KISS

Do I ever want to forget my first virgin kiss?
That scorched me like a thousand suns blazing,
With thousand senses I could barely breathe,
A pause between the breaths filled by the scent of love,
An invisible tattoo on my heart is etched,
No other road has ever traveled there,
And my heart can never forget the way,
For I hold the key to the secret door,
There I fall asleep in the warmth of first kiss,
It was not a sunset kiss, as it dissolved the doubts away,
In the creases of my lips, is your name carved,
And I swear each heartbeat spoke your name aloud,
The first kiss smothered me onto a time that stood still,
Unprepared I fell into its velvety trap willingly,
Losing myself to where I belong,
Addicted now to a lifelong trap.

FLOW OF LIFE

Starts the flow to hug the shore,
The vast chasm with one flow to link,
    River of life
    Flows ever to and fro,
What perishes at one end,
Is reborn at other end,
    Delicate and tender ever throbs with life
    Flows to start anew,
Gnarled and decayed with life's journey
Leaving behind to meet the other end of new dwelling,
    Laughing and celebrating the gentle breeze
    Breezes in life to start anew,
Now is sad and mournful
With clouds of grief,
    Sweeps and sucks
    To an unknown abyss,
The song sung beautifully
Is buried underneath heaviness of sorrow,
    Farewell and welcome,
    The two sides of destination one,
As the nights retires
With its lurking shadows of darkness,

Emerges the morning
With a twinkle of brightness,
The living dies to enjoy the heavenly joys
The dead paves a path for new seeds to sprout,
The elusive permanency eludes
With the magic of the will-o-the-wisp.

FOR YOU ARE MINE

The moments devoured,
By the winter frost,
Leaving behind a heart so numb,
> For what was not mine,
> Was not to be mine.
Ripped and robbed, lying naked,
Of the rosiest dream,
All in vain.
> For what was not mine,
> Was not to be mine.
The raw emotions on a bed of thorn,
Bleeding and crying,
All in vain.
> For what was not mine,
> Was not to be mine.
The summer sun knocks the heart,
Melting away the winter frost,
Striking a chord between winter and summer.
> For what is mine,
> Will always be mine.
To savor the cherished,
To keep you alive,
I peep at heart,

For you are there in my heart,
For years to come till the end.
The nostalgic journey,
Buries the dark and ugly,
Drenches the soul with the love so intense.
For you are mine,
Will always be mine.

FRAGILITY OF RELATIONSHIP

The fabric of relationship,
Woven and interwoven,
With loving fingers,
Fades and frays,
With dissolution and disappointment.

Psychedelic colors,
Kaleidoscopic hues,
Discolors and cause pain,
The raw emotions tear and snap,
Leaving behind a wound that never heals.

The fabric of relationship on a threadbare path,
The naked truth in all its willingness,
Leaves a gaping void to mock ever,
Sucking one, a part of you,
Into a bottomless abyss.

Salvage yourself,
For a brighter tomorrow,
For the weaver above,
Is busy weaving,
A new tomorrow.

IN HARMONY

The tyranny of external,
binds the internal,
 the inward journey,
 paves the way to the golden path,
the silent cries of,
the captive soul,
 giving way to inner callings,
 the darkened corner radiates light,
the clouds of confusion,
the webs of doubts,fades away,
 the fragmented pieces,
 join together,
the hope of new,
bathes the soul,
 washing away,
 the emotional clutter,
Atlast in harmony,
with the existing self.

LAST MESSAGE

My final time was when you hugged me into a tight squeeze,
That fleeting moment, sang the lullabies of cascading
memories,
With a wink I plotted in one tiny precious moment,
To gladly disown, the breathing me,
As the angels came wooing with sweetest breath,
And the borrowed times lay weary in its wake,
The frayed fringes of life scattered into distant far away,
We will unite another time, to start on a blank page,

A magical flight to unburden myself,
To the outstretched arms of the gushing universe,
Dear children love me a one breath more,
But release me softly from each breath of yours,
Do not suffocate me in the cage of your memories,
Let the teardrops do not linger,
I am nothing but a speck of your old fading yesterday,
The life's jugglery plays its mischievous role,
Now am done with my entire task,

A flame of love will always burn in your heart,
A sweet melody of me you will always hear,
From the rustling leaves of a mellowed season,
I have added patterns to your life,

I will speak in a million silent ways,
From the bosom of morning, you will hear the song of dawn,
And the morning nectar, will be yours to drink,
No loss is ever romantic, but the birth of new is the love again,
Let not a question haunts you in its futility,

Let me be a picture of destiny's artist; add no tear to blemish
the picture,
Adorning a canvas throbbing with life,
Within the universe, I wear a garb of eternity,
Having not a naked body to wear,
Thriving beyond skin and bones,
The juices of life, summer dust devour,
A fistful of dust I am in your palm,
I am above the vulnerability of life,

Eternity kisses me with divine grace,
Tonight I shall dine with the celestial guest,
Now I know all about the secret affairs of the naughty moon,
Making love to a different star each night,
And I am the wind fanning their passion,
Day and night is what I wear,
The sunsets are crimson,
As I have sprinkled them with my blood,

The weightless me is wooed,
By the wispy breaths of clouds,
The tears of joy merge with the rainfall,
Floating above with not a shred of load,

Inhaling exhaling the vast universe,
I fit into the master plan of god,
To be one in the magnificent canvas,
The gates of paradise are mine to enter.

LET NOT

Let no shadow chase you for long,
Let no sunshine die in vain,
Let no sunset lingers in gain,
Let not your heart turn to stone,
Let no smile flashes an emptiness within,
Rosy moment of summer may resign,
Let not the hopes of rosy future burn in pyre,
Let a blissful euphoria of a single moment,
Prison your breath for times to come,
Let no visitor of doom knock the revered shrine within,
Live to be alive in each breath,
Do not live to die in each breath,
Let no wounded moment crown the present.
Let no heartache make you its slave.

LOVE LETTER

My love letter travels unmeasured miles and decades,
Until it finds a door of a loving heart,
Doused with inks of pristine love,
Bathed in tears of longing,
Incantations and dreams woven in an illusionary scrawl,
Hungered breath it holds very dear,
Whispers of love in rainbow streaked words,
Like a nomad in a trance, with roused emotions an extra mile
to travel,
Fistful of sunshine stolen at each sunrise,
To light a sunset's trail,
Stumbling upon dawn to dusk in a ceaseless pursuit,
Are my words tamed in a gentle manner?
For it does not stir a heart of a locked door,
Is there ever a love's blossom?
One knock after another, all in vain,
I am broken a bit by bit,
With broken heartbeats without a rhyme, I live by one
breath less,
I heard once a story of a broken star,
Am I piece of that broken star?
Scattered on a weeping path,
A love lost is no ornament to flaunt,
Soiled is your heart, draped in deceit,
Betray is your ornament, I do not hanker for,

Between us there is a vast nothingness, and there grow weeds
in their glory,
I am not going to ever steal a night of yours,
For you are not worth a dream,
Pleasure of Satan is what your heart grabs,
The words of my heart flutter in an anonymous silence,
But will not bleed ever in a weak moment,
You and I have no story to write on our heart,
For your soul reeks and spew ugliness galore,
Like a corpse ready to decompose,
In my brokenness of rollercoaster ride,
I fill every cranny of my broken soul with warmth,
I reach out from me to myself,
And I vowed to love myself in my heart.

MAGIC OF A GOLDEN STRAND

As you said goodbye to the vulnerable me,
Holding me for the last time under the starlit sky,
The evening that echoed of loneliness ahead,
My eyes were heavy with unshed tears,
Leaving me deserted on a lonely road ahead,
As I took a step backward with a bleeding heart,
Noticing a lonely strand of your golden hair,
Ah! That so delicately clung to me lovingly,
Glimmering to seduce a defeated heart,
Leaving my heart entangled with its golden hue,
The dreamer in me awoke despite a saddened heart,
Rewarding new hopes of loving with no end,
With passion heaving, calmness dancing,
Now I vow never to part,
For despite the goodbyes whispered you left a part for me to
love ever,
That I cupped softly in my palm,
Keeping it safely with tender caress,
With whispers and murmurs emotion gush with excitement,
To quench the thirst of a lovelorn heart,
The heart that truly loved,
Ah! Is now beaming with joy,
I fear not now the pain of separation,

For the hair now rest in a box of love's triumph,
That lies next to my pillow,
Breathing promises with its golden silhouettes,
My secret love affair on a road to a dreamy trance,
Now I am lulled by the fragrance of love.

MAZE OF FACELESS MANY

Standing in a motley of sinful many,
In a maze of faceless many,
Murky evening, virtues demise,
A circus of urban life,
Swarming now in a lustful gush, a deluge of faceless many,
A honey dipped tongue of soiled thoughts,
Sincerity tossed, that once nestled in the heart,
Vices dictate, virtues crumble,
I am lost in a maze of faceless many,

Honesty shrunk, now not visible on any face,
Crown of conceit in its glory,
The shameless many glorify the evening,
With raucous laughter of deafening crescendo,
Inflated pride of furtive glances,
Grace of evening trespassed by raunchy titillation,
Crammed of urban angst of hollowed souls,
Tainted now that shuns nothing,
I am one of faceless many,

The bevy of beauties like Barbie dolls,
A rich garment of brocade shimmers in a risqué hold,
On an inviting voluptuous body,
The koeled lined eyes of vacant gazes,
Smiles frozen, a wicked game of passion simmering,

Disposable emotions adorn a fragile moment,
Vanities buried, values suffocate,
Lustful gestures of come hither hints,
I am one of faceless many,

Clamouring maidens in a game of sins,
Gyrating hips designed to please,
Dipped in wanton red noisily air kiss,
The lips are in a haste to surrender,
To indulge in a carnal pleasure,
In a frivolous mood,
Auctioning themselves,
To the highest bidder,
I am one of faceless many,

Clinking of glasses with great cheer,
Slurring sounds of lecherous intentions,
Champagne on ice,
Passion blazing,
unfaithful breaths crown a evening,
That wore a garb of whore,
Naked lust that drools unabashedly,
Masculine colognes discreetly merge with feminine scents,
In a vilest orgy, risqué drawls,
Animals of human race, a beastly quest,
I am one of faceless many,

A lopsided smirk with the cigar dangling,
Devours all in its thick smoke,
The stench of obscenity fills my nostrils,
Reels now the evening hapless,

In a heap less debris, gasps now the evening,
Stripped of its last vestige of respect,
In a faceless many, deceived I am to a promise of utopia,
Desperate I am,
To board a flight to planet perfect.

MEMORIES

I write on my heart,
Ah! with tender touch, loving care,
With hushes and whispers, nestled immortal,
Locked the memories entwined in silky thread,
Ah! that swells rejoicing with lighted heart.

Where fades not the ink,
Yellowed paper shorn not,
Buried not in the melancholy chill,
Ah! In the warmth, in the lap of my heart,
Couched eternally in my heart of singing times,

Where nestles affirmation of ties, of happier times,
Where dark and scarred erased to be forgiven,
Ah! the solitude of heart filled with sweetness to the brim,
Lulled to a lullaby, to dream and dream to sing ever,
Dreaming blissfully to be awaken in a trance,

Where no sunset erases the writing,
No passage of time dims the etching,
No storm devastates the engravings of happy promises,
The fragrance of bygone lingers to delight,
Ah! the sweetenth breadth with a quickened beat,

Counting not the tears shed,
Mourning not the departed dear,
No shadow of remorse drowns the heart,
The robbed heart heavier of sunny memories,
Ah! The blessed heart of happier memories,

Aching times vanishes no vision sees,
Peering deeply to swathe in happiness,
Laughing memories that blushes the cheeks,
Matching not the furrows of worries
Ah! the immortal memories that delights ever.

MY LOVE

Dearest of all sprinkle my heart,
with little water,
and I promise to quench the lips,
that is so thirsty.

Pave my road,
with the sweetest love,
and I promise to weed out,
every weed from your path.

Hide me forever,
from the eyes so prying,
and I promise to drink,
every drop of your sorrow.

Smile for me,
the sunniest smile,
and I promise to brighten,
every shadow of your life.

Love me a little,
with a heart so faithful,
and I promise to feed you,
with a heart so large.

Stay by my side,
at the hour so darkened,
and I promise to hug,
every pain of your life.

Wait for me,
at the end of road,
and hand in hand,
We shall walk to the sunshine together.

NATURE WOOS

Woos the nature, stitching together earth's beat,
Covering the maiden in the awakened morning,.

Sunshine wraps the maiden in a passionate blaze,
Weaving a robe of golden threads.

The thwarted hunger in a bellowing breeze of a new dawn,
Dares to disrobe the maiden just awoke,

Heavy with youth is the ripened bosom of a
sunflower smiling,
A rhythmic lilt beckoning visitors from unseen shores,

Dainty dew in all its translucent might,
Poised prettily in a graceful curve,

Unknown visitors wooed by nature come visiting,
A fiery buzz, a scramble to drink the dew,

The golden tresses of sunshine break free,
Far and above to the clouds that hail.

From the thousand oceans, clouds come with bellyful,
Soaking all with a passionate downpour,

Drenches the maiden in passion,
Gushes forth from the trembling azure sky a rapturous lyric,

The balmy winds are in no hurry,,
Caressing and brushing with a tender whoosh,

The sun god is busy once again weaving a golden robe,,
To cover the maiden of his heart,

Watching secretly is the envious moon,
Stealing a glance in a secret moment,

Sunshine and sunsets mother earth wears,
Sunflowers, roses and many more are its jewels,

When the world is asleep on the silver pathways,
Night encroaches upon the tired passion,

Nature woos in its silent ways.

ODE TO A POET

Penning pages of scented moments,
Sweeps waves of poetic feelings,
Waltz vision of far away expression,
A fragrant moment captured in a bewitching hour,
A silver gown the night wore,
A midnight sparkle as the stars winked in conspiracy,
The lonely moon peeked through the curtain of clouds,
Lending a breath of luster to poetic vibes, racy thoughts stole
the entire silver glow,
In the arms of moon, heart of poet in an insane flutter,
Blessed is the stillness that pulsates in dazzling words,
Desperation of helplessness breathes end in an oasis of
tranquility,
Enthralled moment coyly intrigues a muse,
Delirious are the poetic vibes on fire,
Sensual emotions pour from eyes and lips,
Cascading a mute heart,
The winds cradle a dreaming heart,
Rhythmic sol-fa syllables with dancing vision,
Rising higher to absorb the cloud flecked azure,
Gliding on an unpaved path in a trance,
Entwining words with silken threads of weaver's magic,
That shimmers and glitter like no diamond can,
A timeless treasure of words shaping on a raw sheet,

A celebration of words in a bridal blush,
The words draped and wooed by the gaze of a lover's eye,
Freckles of gold and spray of silver pours with boundless emotions,
Lending a final touch with divine harmony.

ODE TO A SOLDIER

With their shining armour,
Hearts so brave,
With a twinkle in his eyes,
So sure of victory,
To die is what he wishes for a nation so dear,
Marches the olive green,
Sacrificed and slaughtered,
To the altar of some power hungry,
Shattered and wrecked,
The proud widow in grief,

Mutilated in mind, with barren heart,
The anguished cries,
Drenches her sorrow,
Bereft and alone,
By the crafty ways of the power hungry,
With none to share,
With none to wipe the sorrow so great,
As the trumpets blow,
The battle won,
Basks in the victory the power hungry.

Alas! in jubilation the sadness of farewell celebrated,
Forgotten and faded is the martyr,
Dead and buried in the selfish hearts,
That is hungry of the power,

But proud is the widow of a heroic soldier,
Bidding a farewell with eyes moist,
Tries to sail from sunset to sunrise,
Lying awake at midnight hours,
Cries the tears of sorrow clouded eyes,
That blurs the vision of all tomorrows.

ORCHESTRA OF EMOTIONS

Lavish display of emotions on a platter of life's trudge,
An uphill to downhill clamour with no restrain,
My heart is ever ready bearing the weight of your new
found quest,
Tread softly as you are my savior in the playful frolic of life,
I am nothing as you color me with myriad shades of
your whims,
Whole as a vulnerable balloon, puffed up in a fragile
translucent vibrancy,
In the serenity of my being, you gate crash a sleeping heart,

Dear emotions fill my life with sweet jingles,
You are my yesterday and tomorrow,
Every breath inhaled is a slave to your psychotic whim,
And I let myself be used,
Nibble not at my heart in your vilest mood,
Your noose is ever tight, as I watch my last on the
life's canvas,
Wearing you always as you sit in my mind's attic,
A coffin or a bouquet on the playground of my heart's gain,
Chasing always until I fade onto nothingness.

PAINTING A LIFE

Seeking day after day to scale new heights,
Under the wings of sunbeam smiling,
I toiled lovingly with a brush in hand,
Painting a life of joyous beat,

With no smear of black,
No hints of grey,
Each morning glow smiles to a painting of golden hues,
Matching to a new zeal awakened,

With the fall of night,
I dream of another painting in the cozy lap of night's veil,
Vibrating the dreams with hope's lullaby,
Waking me into another day splashed bright,

Painted the destiny with honest sweat,
That cannot rest from a driven force,
Brush in hand painted the day,
The faded colors throb in gathered radiance,

Of different style, different colors, no smudge seen,
Ever in haste was the brush always
Giving a touch of red that blushed,
With tender care and happiness gained,

That moment was mine to enjoy,
As I painted day after day,
With gay abandon,
That mocked the colors of darkness,

Beneath the sunset in the fading glow, emerges a night bereft
of sparkle,
Refusing to dream of another day,
Slept the day with no dreams of awakening,
The rising sun lost its way,

Splashes of black smeared the painting of happier times,
A blackened night of deeper woes,
Foreboding doom,
But the brush in hand refuses to mourn,

Gathering strength with a might to withstand,
To paint a dream to forge ahead,
Yielding not, standing the test of time,
Bids farewell to deeper woes.

POETRY OF LIFE

Somewhere in a drop of tear or in the blush of sun,
Is poetry, I reside,
Sunrise to sunset, consumed I am in a riot of thoughts,
Thoughts are the crutches, rules the roost,
Each breath by breath fills a page of life,
Languishing perfectly on an imperfect to perfect pages,
Pages of life swarm with breaths of past, today n tomorrow,
Sloshed I am in the mysterious flirtiest seasons,
I catch my reflection from the cracks of my heart,
Sadness of an aimless gain and a gainful deluge of joy fill
the pages,

Insanely drunk I am from gain and loss of life's pages,
And I swim from one breath to another with a sigh!
Im born numerous times between each turbulent breath,
Like a star born under the moonbeam,
A luminous birth of another flawless tale,
In the shadows of flickering candle light,
I grope for the new born me;
And I sink gracefully between two weary breaths,
Will people search me in their life's pages?
I know not on which page of their life I will be,
And the poetry of life will unfold with a sweet sigh!

RAINBOW WALKING

My childhood dream of rainbow walking,
Woke me with an innocent kiss of myriad shades,
Red, blue violet, indigo, orange, green, yellow,
Dreams of daylight break of rainbow glow,
Gingerly cradles my body and soul in the seventh heaven,
The ethereal canvas above attired of diaphanous colors,
Infinite path of cascading arch,
An unplanned visit of a magical spell,
From a faraway land of radiance,

I now walk on a rainbow bridge,
Clutching my heart in an excited tremble,
Wearing nothing,
But a hint of smile and giggles,
Cloaked in rainbow's glory,
Merging in oneness in the purity of colors,
My eyes reflecting a mystical connection,
A lover's fantasy of continuous ecstasy,

Clouds of black cape move aside,
Giving a way to garland of colors in an arch,
The fury of sky sees its end,
Thunder and lightning dissolving away,
Rainbow kissed canvas has no cloud of gloom,

Wailing winds, now laughing of joyous vision,
A seductress bows, seizing all in its arch,
Flirting the winds,
Ogling in a rhythmic brilliance,

Time and thought stand still,
In awe of lingering bouquet of nature,
Miles and miles of ribbons interwoven,
In a delicate grace from heaven to earth,
Adam and Eve must have dance their way through,
From heaven to earth,
Passion unfurling,
Tasting fruits of luscious love in unison,

Dear rainbow, where do you come from?
I need no mountain to reach above,
Just a promise of a rainbow,
I will fly like a dragonfly,
To follow to your doorway,
Where the angels sprinkle colors of love,
And the pot of gold will be mine to take,
Between the world,
I dream my dream of fantasy.

REAWAKENING

Now I reshuffle the cards of my life,
Stacked together hands joining,
Restoring the holy cards from a mess of human folly,
A sinful life full of human sorcery,
Unwrapping now to ignite a purest spark,
The new vision sprouts a seed of harmony,
Yes, a harmony to an inner calling,
Bestowed upon by the master builder of human tree,
Whittled life flecked now of a fragrant whiff of awakening,
The tangled shadows of worthless desire decays,
The errant vision now not floundering,
Reborn I am once again,
Holding a chalice of divine longing,
Thirsty love releases a hymn of divine union,
I am humbled now to a life of reward,
Sails now a soul, a conquered life.

ROMANCE AT NIGHT

Steps gracefully the clouds to watch the night's passion,
As floats the lofty moon with its silvery wings,
Embracing in its fold the black velvety sky,
The millionth diamonds dancing away,
Winking and seducing,
The world seized with longing uncontrolled,
The gentle breeze with a sweet moan,
Captivates the flowers in its grip,
The whispering winds nods its approval,
As the swaying trees romances the breeze,
The dancing shadows entwined with grace,
The night's shadow on a passionate trail,
The silence of night murmurs softly a language of romance,
Now is heady with the fragrance of love,
A far off sound of a bird,
Pierces the fullness of romancing night,
The night's passion spent and weary,
Drifting to rest in the lap of morning,
The silvery magic moves aside,
Yet to emerge on another time.

RUINS OF WAR

Palaces echoes of dreary history,
Broken incantation of desperation gasp in debris,
Innocent wails haunt the cavern,
Blood stained walls of a gory past,
A nameless wanders through crumbling remains,
Witches and demon make hay in the smoldering ashes of ruins,
Untold tales languish from each nook and cranny,
Trapped and suffocating in a limbo,
Cracking under hollowed times,
A demise of thousand years,
Lurking in shadows is the muffled moan of sadness,
Painful prison of thousand years with no liberation,
Time and space cloaked with nothingness,
But of heartrending helplessness,
The vampires flaps in the ominous darkness,
Feasting on to the last trickle of blood,
Grief is born of ruins of war.

SILENCE

Grazing not the greener pastures of superficial world,
The external medley of orchestra, a device to fool,
In the silence, fabled happiness of illusionary external,
Do not invade,
A sneak peek to the niche of my soul,
As I wandered in my inner shrine,
I woke up to the resplendent silence,
In that hush there is no forlorn heart,
Where no shadow reaches, as I hug every inch of me,
The heart jingles, the mind waltz,
A harmonious merging of two in love with each other,
The narcissist words surrender meekly,
Within me I have no name, as I meet the real me,
The secret I hold in the treasure box of my silence,
Is nobody's business,
Living not in the people's world of quest,
At last at home with myself within me.

SLICE OF EUPHORIA

Beneath the swaying gulmohar tree,
Passionate blaze, aglow of new revelation,
Raw insight of new vision,
I see not myself, but god mirrored within,
Hugging myself, lured to the love's pursuit,
A fiery lover smoldering within,
Whimsical me delirious in love's candor,

Parched soul on a love sprinkled path,
Nurturing a spiritual garden, a holy sprinkle,
I am a beauty of god's unleashed desire,
A perfect portrayal of god's splendor,
Chanting rhythmically, in drunken euphoria,
Enamored heart beat of your name, in need,
Locked in my love's locket,
Is the warmth of your love indeed?

In the tranquility of my soul,
Spontaneous conversation soaring up of crazy joy,
Chasing transcendental highs of lyrical poise,
An infinite breath of infused togetherness,
Reincarnation of perennial joy,
As I merge,
With almighty alone,

Drinking nectar from god's wondrous infinity,
A pounding heart and dilated pupils,
Heavy with concoction of love and bliss,
The breathless breath seductively merges,
With almighty alone, within myself,
Euphoric moment,
Cannot be tamed,

Selfish to the core, I am one with god alone,
A slave of my inner wanderlust,
Alive with each wonderment,
A spiritual warrior, I am captive to where I belong,
Secret bond in my sacred heart,
A spiritual retreat,
Of my desire alone.

SONG OF HEART

I sing my own song,
The song of heart,
In a conspiracy with the heart willful,
With the treacherous winds on a flight to fancy,,
Sweeping and carrying far and beyond,
Breaking free, embracing my song,
Where the sorrows yield,
Yields to the song of the heart..

Singing my own song,
The song of my heart,
The butterflies swoons to my dictates,
And I steal all their colors,
The honey bees dance to the sweet scent of my song,
The golden rays,
The golden drops,
Showered on to sweeten the song of heart.

Mesmerized and mellowed,
Are the tides that roared,
Lulled by the song so sweet,
Pauses awhile the stormy ocean,
Making way for the song to reach,
Far and beyond to resonate across,
The wings of my heart, spread far and beyond,
Singing the song, the vagabond in me do not rest,

In haste are the cascading waterfalls,
To be in harmony with the song of my heart,
The rainbow stoops,
Streaking my song with the colors so gay,
A gathered radiance by a song so free,
Past and future in rhyming rhapsody,
Singing the song,
The song of my heart,

Where the night is pregnant with million sparkles,
And no day is bare,
A joyous heart of a maddening beat,
Resonates far and beyond,
To the mountains, to the peaks,
And to kiss the stars goodnight,
The clouds guiding to the golden pathways,
And then gather all the sunshine,

Between the sun and moon, I sing my own song.
With no returning, no turning back,
No shadows to fall,
The heart sings, the eyes dance,
The laughing mouth with lips inviting,
Drinking the air in a wildest orgy,
If you hear a sweetest song,
That is the breath of my heart's melody.

SPRING

Darling spring, why do you arrive after a year long wait,
You are my sweetest pain,
As I wait for eternity at a solitary end,
Through treacherous season, I wear a heart of gloom,
The curse of winter laughs in glee,
And my heartbeat echo a melancholy sob,
A winter heart no lover embraces,
And with parched lips i crave for your first kiss of breath,
Dearest spring, you are my love of all seasons.
But you desert me too soon to sleep in the arms of
other seasons,
Love me a little less, but sleep in my heart all the times,
Let no autumn, winter grow in my heart,
Autumn, winter be a garment others wear,
You walk in beauty resplendent with your sweetest chant,
Your secret purpose I dare to intrude,
A barren patchwork sewed by heart beat of gracious spring,
Bare feet and bare heart I chase you wild,
I breathe deep a whiff of you, then to date you each moment,
You grow blossoms in the autumn of a heart and warm a
winter heart.

TEARS

Shhh……do you hear the silent stream?
From the prison of the emerald eyes,
Let the deluge flow in all its grace unabashed,
Caressing the cheeks in gentle streaks,
Are they my friends or foe?
Millions emotions entraps in its hold, mocking and threatening
to an insane rush,
Brimming tears of unspoken words mirrored a
broken summer,
Cradled in the arms of barren autumn of my heart,
Unseen bridge of myriad seasons,
Are these the snuffed screams of anguish?
You fall a prey to changing season,
Laughter, sorrow is all you seek,
Silent whisper of a pearly torrent, in haste to fill an
empty dream,
As they trickle in woes and desire, where the words fail,
Peppered with saltiness is the sigh!
Do I have a deep ocean within? Each tear takes a refuge in its
cocooned warmth,
A heart's capsule, a bridge to my inner most self,
I beg the tears to come when it rains,
For the rain god will drink all my despair,
You do not trickle from rusty windows,
Nor do you come from ruins of past,
You come in guise of calm grace, in your pure innocence,
You are my fragile moments, gift wrapped into a pearly dew,

Past, future all flow in the present,
Behind all the haze and mist, you make a heart crystal clear,
And let grief drown in the little puddle,
You are my soul mate of all seasons,
As I bid adieu to the wails of tears, Angels come to
kiss it away,

THE CRY OF A SOUL

Higher and higher,
To the heaven above,
To the silver sphere,
Cannot add another breath,
At last must part,
From the body to a journey above,

The silence so ominous,
With the smell of death,
Standing alone,
Wretched and wrecked,
Ripped and torn from its body,
The soul crying the parting tears, invisible to all.

The icy mourning sheet so deathly white,
That comforts not the weeping soul,
A painful cacophony of the soul,
Heard by none,
Seen by none,
Breeding a doom, amidst the mournful mortals,

The body lies still, hollow inside,
The hands that held lie helpless,
The lips that kissed are cold and white,

The eyes that promised will never open,
The laughter that filled each corner,
Is a silent echo.

The mother earth in her fury,
Swallows another,
Into her greedy belly,
If she was not so hungry,
You would be forever,
Buried in my heart.

Slowly and silently,
The parting tears,
Flows to years,
To sunset,
To sunrise,
Leaving behind an ache so dull.

THE END

When every sun-rise was your slave,
And the rainbow obliged to color the life gay,
The wandering winds brought laughter at home,
The hearth lit by joys and cares.

Now as you lie in a withered form,
The silent fear took a mighty form,
Weary as you are in a strong hold of pain,
Squeezing a tear to fight the last battle.

The rise and fall of your breath so tired,
Tells a tale of a glorious life spent,
I save each breath, for years to come,
To withstand the loss till I rest.

The clouds thunders the arrival of doom,
Cries the rain the tears of parting,
The living move aside to pave a path for death to arrive,
Death and gloom come holding hands.

A life's fatigue rest in peace now,
But the longing eyes pine for that is no more mine,
Nothing to fear, nothing to lose,
For I have lost that was the dearest.

As you bask in the loving care of almighty,
Smiling at those yet to join,
I trudge along with the weight of pain,
And with loneliness that weeps.

THE WILLOWY LASS

Tall and willowy,
Effervescent and ethereal,
The cloud cloaks the lissome lass,

The azure eyes brims with infinite wonder,
A dive into Misty depth, a window to unravel
A restless virgin heart caged within,

The cool breeze in a flirtiest mood
Fans the passion blazing,
Bare and naked are the raw emotions eager to explore,

A new dawn painted on a canvas of youth,
Made merry, the sun kissed passion,
A bosom, heaving in a "come hither hints",

''The forget me not'' twined with golden tresses,
Hugging and kissing
The bold tresses with honey filled sweetness,

A darting glance by the sun,
Teasing around the golden head,
Lends a golden tiara,

A fictitious love story is daydreaming,
Million stars sparkle in the eyes of the lass,
And the day of passion slips into night of passion,

The ever hungry pout of willowy lass,
Parted and desirous,
To beckon the knights into a magical titillation.

TIME TO SAY GOODBYE

When the heart still yearns,
To relive,
To relish,
The sweetness that was there,
That oozes now with a taste so bitter,
    Time to say goodbye.

When the hidden cries,
Rock the mind,
The emotional binding,
Cracks and break,
Eroding the softness of togetherness spent,
    Time to say goodbye.

When the sunniest smile,
Turns into a ghost of smile,
The heart lies barren,
Naked and jagged,
Stripped of all emotions,
    Time to say goodbye.

When the rosiest dream,
Brutally kicked,
With no traces to dream on,

Shattering an illusion,
Of a rosier tomorrow,
 Time to say goodbye.

When the emotional ambers,
Flicker for awhile,
The silent fire,
That once raged with burning passion,
Reduces now to a heap of ashes,
 Time to say goodbye.

When the fragrance of yesterday,
Reeks out a stench,
The decaying relationship,
Nibbling away at the soul,
Time to bury the past,
 Time to say goodbye.

TRAPPED SOUL

Dwelled once a soul so pure,
With the smile so innocent,
An Armour to win hearts,
The eyes mirrorth,
The pathway to the purest soul,

Rejoiceth the soul,
With the purest thoughts,
Spreading sunshine,
To the hearts so darkened,
A ray of hope to the dreams fallen asleep,

But the road to life,
Have miles and miles to go,
Paved each day,
Layer after layer,
To slain and stain the soul so pure,

Alas! The murky bands entangles the gullible soul,
Lofty egos, layers of ills,
Shuts the window of the soul,
Cages the soul,
With layers of malice,

Sighs and sobs,
Soul tormented,
Weeps the conscious,
Buried and muffled,
In the layers so thick,

Vain are the layers,
Of ambition and conceit,
Of foolish pride, wisdom denied,
Causing pain with no gain,
The trapped soul with no escape,

Alas! Once the soul so pure,
Gasps and chokes,
For a want of pure air,
Burdened and heavy,
With layers of vices,

Oh Lord! Perish the layers in the dust,
Feed my soul with love so divine,
Bathe thy soul with thoughts so pure,
Rock in the lap with the touch so healing,
Lock me in your heart from the world so evil.

TSUNAMI

Come-hither calmness of ocean charmed thy heart eternal,
Beckoning thy heart with a mesmerizing seduction,
Lulled to the brim with desire awakened,
The satiny kiss of the tides flirt the toes,
That curls up in passion in an enchanted moment,
Gold sprayed sand laughs with glee,
Hugging the toes with passion unfolding,
As I stand on a bed of passion to bask in the playful
blueness shore,

The sky bows down lending its azure blue in magnanimity,
Smiles down the sun of golden hues,
The laughing winds caress the tides that rippled in delight,
An indulgent glance by the clouds, never in remorse,
Ah! The nudity bejeweled of dazzling playful tides,
Bobs up and down in swelled pride,
Bobbing evil that hid in swelled pride,
An unknown veiling the fate of mankind unseen,

The eclipsed no vision sights,
The deathly doom ceasing not,
Roars the tsunami with evil design,
A malicious smirk, a hunger so monstrous,

Swallowing all with gushing haste,
An evil vendetta of unknown reason,
Devours the tomorrows of dreams dreamt,
Desire blurs in overshadowed doom,

Ah! The young,
Ah! The old,
Ah! The rich,
Ah! The poor,
The love nest perishes in a watery grave,
Echoes in unison a sadness in eternal drone,
Naked bodies, souls ripped,
Gasps its last to be lost,

Painful moans of desolate torsos,
Sighs for a decent farewell,
What lies now no heart can bear,
The greedy lust of a bellowing belly,
Hissing and panting for its next prey,
Now retreats the tsunami with a satisfied smirk,
Rejoicing the victory with a belch that torments,
The carnage left of brimming wails.

UNDYING LOVE

The day our glances met, I found my piece of missing heart,
That was stolen in a mesmerizing stillness,
You stole my heart when it was ripe,
The deepest secret nobody knows,
For I have too, your heart pounding within me,
Had I trodden a different path,
I would have walked with an vacant heart,
A slave to each, as our hearts echoed in agreement,
In hurricane's eye our love was not a lie,
Your cologne and my perfume filling all crevice of our being,
In your arms I wore nothing but a concoction of passion
and bliss,
What I wear now is your love alone, smelling, only of
your odor,
You made a barren heart grow roses,
Every breath you inhale is a kiss to my heart,
In sagging times our love outshone,
Miles and years cannot rob a love of million promises,
Each night as the hooting of an owl reaches a crescendo,
I fly to unknown destination,
Just to snuggle in your arms,
Our love is poetry,
That will see the passion of million sunrises,
You are my first to be my last,
There is no fairy dust to sprinkle,
Filling the pages of life with undying passion,

If ever you lose your way,
You will find the address in my doting heart,
I know you lied at times, but your flaws are mine to possess,
I am destined to a destiny's addiction,
Now growing old in a far flung miles away,
I am richer with a crumpled photo of you,
Peeping from my threadbare pocket,
A smile flirt the quivering lips,
In a secret hour a peek into my dusty aging dairy,
Amidst the frayed pages sits a rose squinting with a half smile,
A promise of undying love,
I dabble with loving strokes, your name in my heart etched,
With no name to this undying love,
Where time and heart rhymed in harmonious rhapsody,
In the warmth of your love, no night is ever cold.

WHAT I AM WAS NOT

One misty rainy morning,
I was drenched of another me of another time,
Each raindrop mirrored, another me in its dainty hold;
A stranger at crossroad, I do not know,
And I romanticized with each diaphanous bubble of a
tuneless frenzy,
A tryst I was not wedded to,
And it promised never to be my own,
The rain soaked day divulged onto furtive susurration,
The tick of clock fearlessly breathes life into the haughty past,
Leaning on a hazy silhouette, the flitting gaze sees the times
that sailed,
The ballerina of fictitious days dances with million silhouette
flashback,
My heartbeat spiked with zillion glances that glare at me,
And I squirm in its trap,
A fragile heart in clutches of a mind to the days of yore,
Gazing unabashedly the stark nakedness of my past,
No tear or a sigh! And I gaze,
A walk of contemplation, I wear no mask of another me,
Shying not of the nakedness for it brings the best of me,
As I rummage in the debris of me, of a mocking past,
The blurry picture has been edited from time to time in
passionate effort,
A story built in the sand dunes of yesteryears; I do not
sleep beneath,

Once the proud scars, now do not ogle, for I wear it
with finesse,
For what I am, I was not,
O dear! I wear no mask of another me,
Breathing one breath by breath in a lingering heave,
So as not to drown in the deluge of past,
The demons of past are slaughtered with great aplomb,
And the slaying spree sees me basking in bliss,
In a moment of benevolence,
I bequeath my yesterdays to a far flung land of another me,
No more blinded by the sunshine others stole,
For now I have my own sunshine to be luminous within,
The love I gave, to the highest bidder, in a desperate gamble
of emotions,
Is now lost in the labyrinthine alleyways,
Twilight bids a jubilant farewell to empty howls of
yesteryear's juvenile,
My loneliness buried in the catacomb of yesteryears,
Not heavy on my shoulder, do not haunt the cozy nook
of my heart,
Now I arrive a little drunk,
A bit of stardust is sprinkled,
My love potion potent with the scent of spring within me,
Masterpiece created of all seasons of varied hues,
The love of me has not died,
The jaded past do not hiss,
For I nestle in the glow of a new found solitude,
Beneath my black lingerie I reacquaint myself to the
newfound me,
I do a favor to myself,

Liberating myself from the jaunt of yesteryears with
great panache,
For what I am I was not,
And we are not destined to be one,
Together we walked,
But journeyed alone,
For no piece of my today is stolen by yesteryears.

WHERE IS HOME

Was my home in the womb of my mother?
But that was long severed with the umbilical cord cut,
Was my home in the lap of my mother?
But that is where I dreamt away to another home,
Is my home in the niche of my heart?
Tucked deeply, where none dare to peek,
And I frequent a million times,
But that is where vilest visitors of million thoughts,
Slink through devious designs,
Crumbling the sanctity in heap,
Reeking of a stench, a poisoned mind on prowl,
Is my home in the arms of my lover?
But the warmth will linger till I breathe beautiful,
Is my home an address at the end of a street?
With bricks and mortar of cold concrete, to call it one's own,
Stalking the passerby for every attention,
Is my home in the laughter of my children?
But they will abandon the nest in time,
Leaving the aching bones to sigh!
Will my home be in a piece of land?
Where at last my soul will rest in peace,

Where the winds will whistle past in no hurry,
And the epitaph of my permanent abode,
Will glow in the dark,

As the glow worm will blink the address in dark.

WHISPERS AT NIGHT

I hear whispers through the cracks of darkness,
Silently roaring in all its glee,
Silent knocks spook me to death,
Unseen foot fall walks through the alleyways of night,
A flailing soul flitting in the doorway,
Breezy shadows stealthily dancing with diabolic images,
As the inky night spreads its claws and fangs,
And the darkness laughs in an utmost sinister whisper,
Is this laughter of life's decay?
As I wriggle, the bed sheet becomes my noose,
My breaths are not in my command.
Is it a dance of death whispering a name?
I hear no sweet lullaby of night's maid,
Are these the demons of doom celebrating?
In the mute darkness, shadows moan,
And the night slips into the garb of a velvety canopy,
I fall a prey to night's alluring vile tricks,
My shrieks no daylight hears,
Is this a whisper within myself? An eerie silence no daylight
communicates with,
Stalking me faithfully as I crawl in cold sweat,
Encroaching sweet dream of a slumber,
In the calmness of my slumber i lie in nightmare's
ominous trap,

One breath close to hundred years,
And I gasp between the two breaths,
I pinch myself till I bleed red,
Checking to see if I am alive,
Trying not to kiss the phantoms lurking within,
But I hear a whisper and quiver with fear.

WHO AM I

An anonymity given a name that is to dwell upon,
Till the time frays,
A garment of body worn,
Till it wears off to its tattered end,
A pulsating beat to keep me warm,
Till the deaden chill of parting,
Am I an essence of fragrant pollen?
That is windblown from one end to another beginning,
Do I dwell in the whiff of a flowing breeze?
That is to hug million destinations,
Am I a stranded tide of god's will?
That is to journey a zillion shores,
Am I a creation of god's fertile imagination?
That is to taste nectar and ambrosia of countless births,
Am I page in the book of life,
That will decay as the mites will gorge in a devilish flurry,
Am I a body that drapes the soul?
In a tyranny of self possession,
I try to befriend myself, the great lie,
The unfathomable, unknown gropes for a sprinkle of
realization,
I know the answer lies above the sky's garb of cloud.
Where the god is busy spinning fabric of life.

WRINKLES

I stand and look for a very long,
Facing a stranger of raspy breaths,
Misty eyes gazes a cloudy mirror,
 Peering closer and closer, have traveled a long way,
Seeing million lines crisscrossing in a conspiracy,
Like a chameleon in a flower shrub,
Shrouded in its own ugliness,

Trying to find myself in the reflection of yesteryears,
Holding a gaze in a haze, all in vain,
A trace of self lost, in a mesh of lines, of pain and laughter,
Scars of years, strangulated amidst the spider web,
Bewilderment locked within, a gibberish gab of
incoherent rant,
Crackling and cursing the mirror with utmost might,
The vengeful mirror mocks with a snigger, once so loyal is in
a guise of a traitor,

The lips with creases,
Like a rose petal crushed on,
Deathly pallor of skin like a rotten apple,
Laughter line of it's over indulgence,
Once well coiffured head is an unruly mess,
Tousled wispy strands emits a silver streak,
Wisdom gained, that is wise beyond years,

The cheeks are like a balloon sucked, of its last breath,
Do I see my fate in bumps and folds of my face?
That is lined with, harmonious crisscross lines,
An amazing work of an artist of deft strokes,
Each line has an emotion engraved with tender care,
Paving a path,
To the secret garden of my heart,

The deepest secret, the mystery of life lived of all seasons,
Hidden in each grace of wrinkle, a rippling emotion,
Despairing not, for all the treasure of wisdom,
Is mine to possess,
Although I am robbed by a thief invisible,
But the epiphany can crush not confidence of today,
Adorable I am,
On a threshold of a new beginning,
Old wine in a new bottle,

Walking the twilight of my sunset trail,
Stopping at the end of road,
To watch the sunset in its proud glory,
My flagging spirits are nowhere at sight,
As each day adds to be born as a year,
I chose to live without an expiry date,
I am at home after years of aimless wander,
In a cozy smugness of new understanding,
I would die young at my rocking ninety,
With a glass of champagne celebrating life.

YESTERDAY ONCE MORE

Prays the feeble heart to enjoy more of yesterday,
Trembles the lips to hear a loving word,
Stretches the hand for a tender touch,
Fall not a tear, for there is no one to wipe,
Hides each wrinkle the pain of neglect in its fold,
The great task done, the life at its end.

Yesterday once more, sighs the heart.

I am one of many thousands in oblivion,
Long forgotten the victories,
The sacrifices seen their funerals,
The faithful shadows of darkness hovers with a
loyalty so dark,
The foul mood of a frosty wind,
Lashes out to the aching joints.

Yesterday once more, sighs the heart.

The nights are full with lurking fears,
The days are empty with vacant gaze,
But the treasured memories fill the heart,
Where every joy,
Where every sorrow,
Embraces the other.

Yesterday once more, sighs the heart.

The sinking sun dares in a last attempt,
To spread its dying sunshine,
What gushes forth the emotions unchecked,
Where the distant flute plays,
On a path that was traveled,
That lacked not its share of joys and sorrows.

Yesterday once more, sighs the heart.

The fleeting visions visit more and more,
When the eyes sleep to dream for more,
But the heart wakeful with immortal memories,
The borrowed time mocks at all times,
But age does not wither the immortal memories,
That I will share with almighty alone.

YOUTH

Now I board a plane of thoughts,
To tinker with the mesmerizing youth,
A journey millionth times in one journey, of hormone
filled days,
Stirring up youth's galore and vices to spill,

Snuggling deeper to a journcy of dalliance,
Treading softly in the wilderness of youth,
Clearing cobweb in a long lost alley,
The secret alley opens up to another alley of youth's
indulgence,

Flirted the youth brazenly with no stopping,
Trading the soul for a psychedelic high, to a marijuana smoke,
A shameless dance of youth's exuberance,
The fizz of Champagne was no match to the oozing youth,

Slithering silently with a sweet poison,
Hedonistic indulgence of sly ways pile up,
Treacherous ways to dark alleys,
Scattered sanity in the dumps,

The efflorescence youth knew no limits,
Squandering life of all its energies,
With no sanctity, grabbing all in haste of greed,
Like there is no tomorrow,

The wilderness of youth had many hearts broken,
Naïve as I was, to fall in the youth's craftiness,
My heart was captive, only to shatter in thousand pieces,
Each piece reflected my broken heart; with a nasty twitch I came alive,

The scars diminished, the voices of temptation muted,
As I delve deeper, counting the broken hearts,
Rejoicing with a conquered smirk,
I have journeyed through thousand sunsets,
To be worth a million sunrise.